C000024464

THE LIFE & TIMES OF

Henry VIII

BY
James Brown

This edition first published by
Parragon Book Service Ltd in 1996

Parragon Book Service Ltd
Unit 13–17 Avonbridge Trading Estate
Atlantic Road, Avonmouth
Bristol BS11 9QD

Produced by Magpie Books,
an imprint of Robinson Publishing

Illustrations courtesy of: Bridgeman Art Library;
Hulton Deutsch; Peter Newark's Historical Pictures

ISBN 0 75251 586 1

A copy of the British Library Cataloguing in Publication
Data is available from the British Library.

Typeset by Whitelaw & Palmer Ltd, Glasgow
Printed in Singapore

PRINCE HENRY

'Get sons' might have been a king's motto in the fifteenth century. Sons were crucial in the world into which Prince Henry was born. His father, Henry Tudor, had established himself, for want of better, as the Lancastrian claimant to the throne, and won it at the Battle of Bosworth. Having married one of the principal surviving claimants in the rival branch of the royal family, Elizabeth of York, Henry VII had the luck to sire two sons, and several daughters. Under the system of primogeniture the throne would pass to the oldest surviving son and only when there were no sons would the daughters be considered. In a violent world – a male world – the succession of a woman to the throne was deemed a recipe for disaster. If she married a prince of her own rank, he would have to be a foreigner; such a husband would, in effect, rule the kingdom. If she married one of her own noblemen, then there was a risk of factionalism dividing the kingdom, as one noble family would then be likely to monopolize patronage, and the only hope for those excluded would be by resorting to strife.

In many ways it was a deeply conservative world, which was partly why it believed in succession by blood. The idea of a popular

Henry VIII by Joos van Cleve

democratic election to determine who held power would have been incomprehensible to many, and absurd to most. How could the many-headed monster of the people be expected to agree about anything, least of all about who should lead them? The people needed to be led: that was what they were born to. That some were born to rule and some to follow was part of an established order. The Church and the King between them commanded the loyalty of the people, not because they had competed for it against some rival system, and not (as would become clear in the course of Henry VIII's reign) because they necessarily agreed with one another. They did so simply because they were part of the established order and had always commanded the allegiance of the majority because there was simply no alternative.

3

People might wish that this or that were otherwise, but not that the whole system be otherwise. By the end of Henry's reign he had brought the latter wish a degree closer to being readily conceivable. But it was not a potent one in the century in which he had been born.

In England the fifteenth century saw civil war: the Wars of the Roses, the collective name for a series of battles fought between 1455 and 1485. The struggle was primarily a dynastic one however. There was little at stake in terms of ideas and general policy: what was being contested was who should be king, not whether there should be a king. That would be among the questions contested in the later Civil War in the mid-seventeenth century, during which Charles I would be tried and executed, with the result that England was ruled during the 1650s without a king. But that was a very different kind of war being fought in a very different world – a world that was just being born during the reign of Henry VIII.

Henry lived for just over fifty-five years; he was to be king for nearly forty of them. However, he was not born to rule. He was only the second son of the King. It was expected that his elder brother, Prince Arthur (so called because his father wanted to shore up his questionable claim to the throne with some Arthurian kudos), would succeed. As a younger son, Henry didn't matter much, and so from the date of his birth (28 June 1491) until Arthur's early death in 1502 relatively little is recorded of him. His name appears from time to time as honours were heaped upon his young shoulders, but where there was any work involved in these appointments it was done by a deputy. The accumulation of titles, which would be the outward signs of an illustrious career in anyone else's case, merely underlined the distinction of royalty.

With the death of Arthur his position changed. Suddenly he was heir to the kingdom his father had won and the considerable treasure he was accumulating. He inherited his brother's position, his titles of Prince of Wales and Duke of Cornwall, and eventually his wife. Catherine of Aragon was the daughter of one of the most powerful and devious men in Europe: Ferdinand II, King of Spain. Princes and princesses seldom married for love, and they usually married each other. Royal marriages were counters in the game of international power play. The plans for Henry and Catherine's marriage were set forth in an international treaty between England and Spain. Signed in 1503, it agreed that Henry would marry Catherine in the year after his fourteenth birthday (two years in the future), while Spain would supply 100,000 crowns' worth of jewels and plate as dowry. There was a slight snag: a couple of passages in the Old Testament were widely taken at the time to prohibit a man marrying his brother's widow. However there were two ways round the problem. Her marriage to Arthur could be discounted on the grounds that it had never been consummated or, on the assumption that it had, a special dispensation could be sought from the Pope to allow her second marriage to go ahead anyway. The latter was the course agreed upon between England and Spain: neither wanted to leave a loophole which the other side could exploit in order to have the marriage annulled at a later date!

For the time being, the union was still several years away, and Henry was still a child. Little is known of his education, though in the light of his later attainments it must have been intensive. It doubtless included Latin, to which Henry would later add a smattering of Greek. He could speak French and Italian, was a talented musician and composer, expert on the lute, able to play the organ, and something of a singer besides. As a young man he was athletic, possessed of enormous zest and energy, and reckoned one of the handsomest princes in Europe. Perhaps the most significant element in his upbringing was its repressive-

Henry playing a musical instrument

ness. As a man he would be one of the most ostentatious of monarchs, but while his father was alive he seems to have been almost wholly under his father's thumb. Unlike Arthur, he was given no taste of political responsibility. One Spanish diplomat noted that in public he never spoke save as his father directed, while in private he could not have been approached without his father's knowledge, since the way to his rooms lay through the King's. But the discipline his father imposed upon him would not long survive.

KING HENRY

Henry VII breathed his last on 22 April 1509. The issue of his son's marriage was still unresolved, for 28 June 1505, the earliest date stipulated in the treaty for the marriage, had long since come and gone. Henry VII had started to consider alternative brides, even having his son swear that he was having nothing to do with Catherine. Henry VIII's succession to the throne however brought a radical change in policy. A somewhat startled

Spanish Ambassador suddenly found himself in favour, and hastily had to ready his princess for marriage. The obstacles that Henry VII had made much of weighed little with his son.

The marriage was solemnized on 11 June 1509. Catherine was some four years older than her husband, but still young and attractive. The youthful Henry VIII seems to have thought so, for he was to remain married, and, so far as one can judge, attached to her for longer than would be the case with any of his subsequent wives. Even when his affection for her waned, it was only when it became clear that Catherine would never conceive the son he needed that he would set about trying to divorce her.

His father had accumulated 1¼ million

pounds' worth of gold, plate and jewels, earning himself the reputation of an extortionate miser in the process. Henry VIII promptly set about shedding his father's reputation along with a hefty portion of his money. He was particularly prodigal when it came to ceremonies. For his coronation, courtiers and horses were decked in extravagant, bejewelled costumes, and the junketing continued for several days. Henry VIII was inordinately fond of jousting, and, though he did not participate on this occasion, proud of his prowess. Another tournament featured among the celebrations that marked the birth of his short-lived (as it turned out) son on New Year's Day 1511. Such was Henry's vulgar largesse that he allowed the crowds to pluck off the golden letters H and K (for Henry and Katherine) that adorned his splendid clothes.

Catherine of Aragon

The first years of the new reign also gave the world its first taste of the all too real violence that would become its hallmark. In raising money Henry VII had employed two servants in particular: Sir Richard Empson and Edmund Dudley. They had made themselves singularly unpopular, and Henry VIII lost little time in gathering complaints against them. Ignoring the manifest fact that they had just been obeying orders, in 1510 he had them executed on a trumped-up charge of treason. The long sequence of judicial murders started early.

Henry VII had pursued a policy of peace. This was no doubt partly because it was much cheaper than war, which was the traditional occupation of princes and their nobles. However, the new king cared little for the cost of war, but craved the glory of victory.

Two obstacles blocked his path. First, he had inherited from his father a Privy Council that opposed war. Second, England was not one of the major European powers. Europe was dominated by three powers – the Holy Roman Empire, France and Spain. Spain and the Empire were dynastically linked, and in due course the Archduke Charles, grandson of the Emperor Maximilian I, as also of Ferdinand of Spain, would inherit them both, but otherwise the shifting alliances of states jockeying for power were regulated either by complex diplomacy or by battle. However, France and the Habsburg bloc (of which the Holy Roman Emperor was the head) were the superpowers – something reflected in the fact that it was northern Italy which became the main war zone of the era. The politics of sixteenth-century Europe was a difficult and treacherous game to play, as Henry would find out. However, it was also the arena in which any international reputation had to be made.

Apart from glory itself, Henry wanted to regain the huge possessions that English kings had once held in France. The so-called Hundred Years War had been in reality a series of intermittent attempts to retake them, but since then all save Calais had been lost. In effect Henry wanted to continue the Hundred Years' War.

For some three years the new king strained at the leash, anxious to wage war on the doddering Louis XII of France, but restrained by his Privy Council. Then events turned his way. His father-in-law, Ferdinand of Spain, with the French king and the warlike Pope Julius II, had formed the League of Cambrai in order to loot the rich independent city-state of Venice and share the spoils. The first part of the plan went well, but when it came to sharing, the French were not having it. Ferdinand and Julius, irked, turned upon their ally. Louis foolishly reacted by challenging the Pope's authority over the French Church. In an age in which almost all of Europe, including England, was Catholic, to fight the French was now a religious duty, and those clerics on the Privy Council who had vetoed war thus far could hardly stand in the way of Henry's desire to obey the Holy Father.

In June 1512 the Marquess of Dorset set sail for France with an army, expecting to join forces with the Spanish and attack Bayonne. He arrived to find no Spanish. Ferdinand waited until French forces had been diverted to deal with the English, and then, rather than help his ally, occupied the Kingdom of Navarre on his northern border. The English troops were badly organized, soaked by rain, short of food and ill. They finally mutinied, hired ships, and went home.

Having allowed the Spanish Ambassador to give his officers a contemptuous dressing down, Henry launched another campaign in 1513. This time the Holy Roman Emperor, Maximilian I, was to join the alliance. The idea was that France should be simultaneously attacked on several fronts by Henry, Maximilian, Julius and Ferdinand. Ferdinand, however, backed out, having made a separate and secret peace with Louis. Even so, Henry embarked with his army for Calais. After three weeks of pageantry, eleven days and forty miles later they arrived at Thérouanne, and laid siege to it.

When Maximilian finally arrived Henry suffered another setback. The Imperial army was much smaller than had been promised. However, Maximilian knew how to manipulate the young king: he offered to put himself and his forces under Henry's overall command. Thus flattered, Henry found that he could stomach having to pay for his ally's army. Shortly afterwards Thérouanne fell. Henry gave the town to Maximilian, who razed it to the ground.

They then proceeded to Tournai, which gave in more readily. After further junketing Henry went home.

Henry's expedition was an improvement on Dorset's, but its achievements paled into insignificance by comparison with events at home. Henry had left Catherine in charge. Scotland was then an independent kingdom, and apt to seize the chance to attack presented by the absence of an English army on the Continent. True to form, James IV marched south. Catherine sent a smaller army under the Earl of Surrey to meet him. On 9 September 1513 they fought at Flodden, just south of the border in Northumberland: by the end of the day Scotland was 10,000 souls the poorer, and among the dead were many a noble and the king himself. Scotland was England's for the taking. Henry, however, was busy elsewhere – celebrating his lesser exploits.

WOLSEY'S RISE

Such success as Henry's expedition had
enjoyed was largely attributable to his
almoner, a cleric who was pursuing a career
in political service. He was hugely
ambitious, intelligent and hard-working. It
was he who had organized Henry's army,
keeping it fed, supplied, moving and
obedient. He did well out of the venture,
for once Tournai had fallen Henry made
him bishop of it. Considering that he was
the son of an Ipswich butcher, Thomas

Cardinal Wolsey

Wolsey had done well for himself. But not half as well as he was going to do . . .

Wolsey offered Henry freedom from the chores of government. When other counsellors urged Henry to pay more attention to affairs of state, Wolsey suggested he pay less. This advice 'delighted him so much and caused him to have greater affection and love for the almoner . . .'. Wolsey's swift promotion was assisted by some of his seniors on the Privy Council, who hoped to retire from politics and saw Wolsey's broad shoulders as being capable of taking over their burdens. They could scarcely have anticipated how central Wolsey would become to government.

As Henry roamed the countryside hunting or whatever, Wolsey stayed in or near

London. Messengers went back and forth between them, as Wolsey tried constantly to get Henry to read at least the summaries that he had made of important documents, to sign papers, and to answer letters. In effect Wolsey's household became the government, but his authority derived solely from the King, who rewarded him handsomely, making him Lord Chancellor, Archbishop of York (1514), Bishop of Bath and Wells (1518), Abbot of St Albans (1521), Bishop of Durham (1523) and of Winchester (1528). He was also made Cardinal (1515) and Papal Legate (1518) by Pope Leo X. Taken along with fees and other moneys, at the height of success he probably had an income of about £50,000, out of which to indulge a passion for ostentation that almost rivalled his master's.

Wolsey gave most of his attention to foreign affairs. It was the area in which Henry most desired to shine, but Wolsey, no less than his king, was glad of an international stage on which to display his talents. In the immediate wake of his coming to power Wolsey applied himself to outwitting Maximilian and Ferdinand. Another concerted campaign against France had been planned for 1514, but Maximilian had, like Ferdinand, covertly made peace with Louis XII. Wolsey saw England's advantage in playing the same game, and secured a better alliance with France than the others; French money, security of possession of Tournai, and an arranged marriage between Louis and Henry's younger sister, Mary.

Things proceeded as planned. Mary was a

noted beauty; Henry persuaded her to shackle herself to the ageing Louis by promising that she could marry whom she wished once she was a widow. Louis obligingly expired within three months of his nuptials. But new perils lay in wait for Mary. Wolsey wanted to keep her as a diplomatic pawn – perhaps to marry her off to the Archduke Charles, who was heir both to Ferdinand and Maximilian. The new French king, Francis I, also had designs on her. However, she was ready to take her brother at his word, for she had fallen for the handsome Charles Brandon, sometime companion of Henry, and Duke of Suffolk, who had escorted her to France. Secretly they married and went home to face the king.

Francis's succession to the French throne

was a thorn in Henry's side. A rivalry swiftly developed between them that was partly personal. Like the young Henry, Francis cut a glamorous figure. But he was also devious enough to play he international game, skilful in war, and king of one of the great powers. In September 1515, having created diplomatic entanglements to keep Henry occupied, Francis's army had crossed the Alps, won Milan, and defeated a Swiss army (the Swiss were the mercenaries of Europe and their soldiership was generally esteemed). Francis had concluded a peace with the Pope on his own terms. Henry, who had boasted that Francis could not cross the Alps without Henry choosing it, had been eclipsed.

In January 1516 Ferdinand died, and was succeeded by his grandson (and also the grandson of Maximilian), the Archduke Charles, who thereby became Charles I of Spain. Charles, Maximilian and Francis then concluded a league of mutual amity, the Treaty of Noyon, which pointedly shunted England to the margins. Wolsey's plans for an anti-French alliance were wrecked. To add insult to injury, Maximilian managed to double-cross the English, cheating Henry out of a hefty subsidy in the process.

However, Wolsey had even more ambitious plans in store. He conceived the idea of winning peace in Europe not by the usual method of one big power trying to dominate, but by a treaty of mutual, collective security between states. Of course the scheme pandered to the vanity of Wolsey and his patron, Henry, who liked to think themselves the arbiters of Europe. But it was also a bold, largely original idea, which won plaudits from many a Christian humanist. After months of painstaking and ingenious negotiation, the Treaty of London was celebrated in October 1518 by a High Mass in St Paul's Cathedral attended by Henry VIII.

The treaty revived earlier plans for a grand meeting between the kings of England and France. The idea was to heal old wounds; what transpired was an unparalleled display for pageantry. The meeting of the Field of the Cloth of Gold was set for 1520. Maximilian had died in 1519, and Charles of Spain had been elected to succeed him as Emperor Charles V by a handful of electors, hereditary German princes. On his way to his possessions in the Low

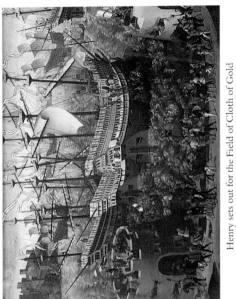

Henry sets out for the Field of Cloth of Gold

Countries, Charles stopped off in England for some quiet, businesslike talks with Henry. The contrast with what followed could scarcely have been greater.

For the meeting of the kings, a miniature artificial city of exotic and costly tents were erected in a field in northern France, near Calais. After an initial tense moment when they and their formidable entourages first clapped eyes on one another, they spent a fortnight dancing, singing and jousting. Finally they parted, agreeing to build a chapel dedicated to Our Lady of Peace on the spot, as a permanent sign of what had been achieved.

The chapel was never built, underlying tensions and old habits reasserted themselves, and England was soon fighting France again.

Wolsey's great treaty lay in tatters as the fractious, bloody dance of European diplomacy resumed, and allies were embraced and betrayed after the usual fashion. Charles V toiled unceasingly, and had the benefit of huge resources. By the late 1520s he had wrested control of northern Italy from France, and his troops had got as far as Rome, where they pillaged the Holy City in May 1527. Henceforth he would be able to exert enormous pressure on the Pope. England was as far from being the major player in Europe as she had been when Henry became king, and his father's fortune had been squandered to no advantage.

. . . AND FALL

Henry may have craved success on the international stage, but in the 1520s he felt more and more driven to tackle an issue of domestic policy – he had no legitimate son. He had exercised his *droit de seigneur* and taken one of his wife's ladies-in-waiting, Elizabeth Blount, as his mistress, and she had borne him a son in 1519. Of Catherine's repeated pregnancies, only one child survived: Mary, born in 1516. Finally Catherine ceased to conceive. There was

Mary I, daughter of Henry and Catherine
of Aragon

some attempt to keep hope alive by medical means, but to no avail.

Henry could be cruel and, by any reasonable standards, unprincipled, but he was no Machiavellian cynic. In many ways he was a devout man, with an urgent need to square his actions with his conscience. That was scant protection for anyone who got in his way, however: Thomas More, when asked whether he did not value the king's friendship, observed that if his head could win Henry a castle in France it would be soon struck off. What More did not mention was that Henry would probably have persuaded himself that he was right to trade a friend's life for a castle.

This nagging conscience was perhaps the reason why one expedient solution,

Sir Thomas More

evidently considered, was not pursued. In 1525 Henry's illegitimate son, Henry Fitzroy, was created Duke of Richmond, which suggests that his father might have toyed with making him his heir. But nothing came of it, and at about this time Henry's capricious conscience began to trouble him on a different score. He cast his mind back to the papal dispensation he had required in order to marry Catherine in the first place, and began to suspect that the reason he had no son was that he had unwittingly committed the obscure sin of marrying his brother's widow, without having had proper dispensation. His erratic conscience may have been spurred on by a growing obsession. Mary Boleyn, the daughter of minor gentry, had briefly been Henry's mistress. Her sister Anne, however, declined to play the usual game when Henry's attentions turned to her. She held out for marriage.

With Henry in this state of unusual animation, Wolsey's life became difficult. He was accustomed to dealing with a monarch too fond of his own leisure to do more than stipulate the broad outlines of policy. Suddenly he wanted something specific: annulment of his marriage to Catherine. Unaccustomed to the idea that his will had any limits, he expected Wolsey as his servant and a Prince of the Church to get what he wanted. Many of his own political servants were churchmen who were paid out of Church revenues for the service they did their king. Cardinal Wolsey was merely the greatest of them.

Wolsey convened a secret tribunal in 1527.

Henry VIII by Holbein

The idea was to review the evidence, establish a case for annulment, and then have the marriage dissolved by Rome before Catherine or her immensely powerful family could realize what was happening and block it. Luck ran out when news reached Wolsey of Charles V's sack of Rome. The Pope, Clement VII, from whom the annulment would have to come, was now under the control of Catherine's nephew, and would be loath to anger the Emperor by disgracing his aunt. Henry also let the cat out of the bag by telling Catherine to her face that in his view they had never properly been married. He compounded this *faux pas* by letting Catherine outwit him and get word of her plight to Charles. However, it was never Henry's way to blame himself when there was anyone else to blame, and Wosley felt even more keenly the pressure of his master's frustration.

Throughout the death-ridden summer of 1528, as people dropped with the sweating sickness, and Henry kept on the move in his urgent efforts to save himself from the disease, he kept firing letters off at Wolsey. Now that the intention was public knowledge and Charles occupied Rome, Wolsey faced huge obstacles. Ideally he would have liked the Pope to give him the powers to deal with the case in England. This he never managed, but he did succeed in having the commission set up to enquire into the case, transferred to England. This would make it possible to put pressure on Catherine to come to terms.

However, the Pope was still anxious not to

offend Charles, and so was playing for time. Proceedings could not begin until Cardinal Campeggio had arrived in England from Italy, and he took his time. When he finally arrived Henry was eager for the hearings to begin immediately, but Campeggio decided that he ought to play marriage counsellor and tried to reconcile the royal couple. He then came up with an ingenious suggestion for which there was some obscure precedent: if Catherine entered a nunnery she could be declared dead to the world, thus making Henry a widower enabling him to remarry. Catherine, however, was having none of this: marriage, she declared, was her vocation.

To make matters worse for Henry, Catherine was popular – as he discovered late in 1528 when they walked together through a gallery linking Bridewell Palace and Blackfriars. The public gave Catherine such vocal support that Henry ordered they be kept out in the future. He attempted a more subtle public relations exercise shortly after by summoning some of the country's élite to Bridewell, and explaining that, but for theological problems, there was no one he'd sooner be married to than Catherine. Henry, however, by this time had taken several mistresses and was increasingly besotted with Anne Boleyn.

Meanwhile Campeggio got to work. Wolsey wanted to show that there were flaws in the original papal dispensation which invalidated it. All parties were accordingly thunderstruck when Catherine suddenly produced a copy of a different papal document dealing with the same

Anne Boleyn

matter. Not only was Campeggio not empowered to investigate this papal brief, but it also seemed to make good some of the alleged shortcomings of the bull. The original of the second document was safely in Charles V's keeping in Spain, which, the best efforts of the English notwithstanding, was where it stayed.

Catherine followed this up with an emotional personal appeal before Campeggio's commission, in the presence of her sullenly impassive husband, for the hearing to be revoked to Rome and then swept out, refusing to return, though summoned thrice. Campeggio had the excuse he needed and announced that since this was a papal court, they would follow the papal terms, and accordingly adjourned for the long summer vacation.

Before it could reconvene the following October, the Pope's order for the case to be revoked to Rome had arrived. Glad to wash his hands of the whole distasteful business, Campeggio departed.

Wolsey must have wished he too could have disentangled himself from the King's 'great matter' as easily. His failure to secure the annulment exposed him to the hostility of a faction of noblemen who resented him as a low-born upstart, as well as for his wealth and position. In September 1529 the Dukes of Norfolk and Suffolk came to him demanding the Chancellor's Great Seal. At first Wolsey refused to believe they were acting on the King's orders, but once this was confirmed he broke down and wept. Two days after being required to resign as Lord Chancellor, Wolsey contrived to come to court, and the King favoured him with two long conversations – to the dismay of his aristocratic enemies. However, they had Anne Boleyn on their side, who resented Wolsey for his part in preventing her earlier intended marriage to the son of the Earl of Northumberland. It is possible that it was she who was finally able to swing Henry against his minister.

Even so, it was still unclear whether Wolsey would be disgraced, or would simply have to retire, perhaps to be rehabilitated in due course. Henry pardoned the Cardinal on one charge that had been brought against him, but the process of stripping him of his wealth and offices continued. For a time it seemed that he would be allowed to retire to his archdiocese of York, but his enemies finally persuaded Henry to have him arrested for treacherous secret dealings with foreign powers. He died at Leicester Abbey on 29 November 1529 while travelling south to stand trial, declaring at the last, 'Had I but served God as diligently as I have served the King, he would not have given me over in my grey hairs.'

THE BREAK WITH ROME

By 1530 Henry had been trying to secure a divorce from Catherine for three years, and it seemed less likely than ever that he would get it. There was another option: if Rome would not give him what he wanted, get it from somewhere else. The German reformer Martin Luther, having started his campaign against abuses within the Church, had ended up leading a religious movement entirely outside the Roman Catholic orthodoxy, and for a variety of reasons a number of German princes had embraced Lutheran Protestantism. The birth of Protestantism would prove to be a turning point in Western Christendom, and it was largely thanks to Henry that England ended up in the Protestant camp. But such a solution seemed singularly unlikely even in 1530. His choice of successor to Wolsey as Lord Chancellor was a man of noted devoutness, Sir (now Saint) Thomas More. Though not a cleric, More had stipulated on reluctantly taking office, that he should not be required to act contrary to his beliefs, and Henry had reassured him that he should 'look first unto God'. In religion the King was fairly conservative. In 1521 he had refuted the Lutheran heresy personally in his theological treatise *Assertio Septem Sacramentorum* (*The Defence of the Seven*

Sacraments), for which an admiring and grateful Pope Leo X had awarded him the title '*Fidei Defensor*' (Defender of the Faith). The title delighted him and his successors retain it to this day, with the letters FD still appearing on British coins.

However, Henry could hope to influence the Pope by putting pressure on the Church in England. While there was scant support for Protestantism as such, there was considerable unfocused resentment of the clergy's wealth, power and privileges. The Church owned a third of the country, and even so it levied tithes in every parish, along with other fees; clergy were not even subject to the royal law courts, but were tried separately. In the parliament summoned in 1529, which would come to be known as the Reformation Parliament, there was sufficient anti-clerical feeling for Henry to direct it to his advantage. Parliament had started by raising questions about activities of the clergy that were incompatible with their religious duties, and, by the end of 1530, Henry was putting increased pressure on the Church by reviving an obscure legal practice, and issuing a writ of *Praemunire* against a group of clerics. It was a semi-defunct procedure for prosecuting clergy who had allowed their loyalty to the Church to interfere with the loyalty they owed their king. The law was so vague that Henry could wield it as he wished. Sensing an opportunity, he extended the writ to cover the whole of the English Church, and in January 1531 the clergy pleaded guilty, and suffered a hefty fine: the convocations of Canterbury and York paid £100,000 and £18,000 respectively.

Henry in middle age

Henry's attack on the Church came to be co-ordinated by the man who replaced Wolsey. Thomas Cromwell was another commoner, and as such resented by a faction of the aristocratic old guard. He had a background in international trade, which he left to join Wolsey's household in 1520. There he served an apprenticeship in government, and after Wolsey's fall from office in 1529, had himself elected to Parliament in the same year. From there he joined the Privy Council in 1531, and over the next few years established himself as the King's first minister. He was instrumental in radically extending the challenge to the Church in Parliament's Supplication, which it made to Henry in 1532, and that challenge was duly passed on to Convocation, the Church's Parliament. It required them to submit all new laws for the king's approval, to have established laws vetted by a Royal Commission, and to acknowledge that the authority of Convocation's laws derived not from the Pope, but from the king. By no stretch of the imagination could this be seen as aiming merely at the reform of particular abuses: Henry sought unprecedented royal authority over the Church. The clergy rejected it, but when the issue was forced, they offered a qualified submission on 15 May 1532. It was too much for Thomas More, on the following day he resigned the Lord Chancellorship.

Though Henry had decided to establish royal supremacy over the Church by 1530, the implementation proceeded by fits and starts. Possibly Henry himself was unsure how complete he wanted the break to be:

perhaps he still hoped to retain some formal connection with Rome. When William Warham, the Archbishop of Canterbury, died in August 1532, Henry appointed a comparatively unknown cleric, Thomas Cranmer, as his successor; but he still sought papal confirmation of the appointment. However, he was driven by the urgent need to beget an heir.

Anne Boleyn had appeared in public in 1532 virtually as the Queen, and had been raised to the peerage in her own right as Marquess of Pembroke. It's possible that this diminished her resistance, for probably in December 1532 she conceived. Now Henry had to act fast, since the child would have to be legitimate, or all would have been in vain. On 25 January 1533 he and Anne were married secretly in Whitehall, the palace which Henry had wrested from Wolsey. In April Catherine was advised that she was no longer the Queen, but merely the Princess-Dowager. The following month, Cranmer convened a secret court at Dunstable to consider Henry's marriage to Catherine. After just four hearings Cranmer pronounced it annulled, and soon afterwards declared the marriage to Anne valid. It is one of the ironies of the situation that Henry's marriage to Anne can be considered to be invalidated by exactly the same passage from the Bible as that invoked to annul his first marriage, for Henry had slept with Anne's sister Mary before marrying her. Later he would invoke this when he wanted to be rid of Anne, but for the time being Anne was anointed and crowned Queen in Westminster Abbey on 31 May.

Princess Elizabeth, later Elizabeth I

The die was cast. The Pope ordered Henry to take Catherine back on pain of excommunication. Henry set about consolidating his position with a series of Acts of Parliament, driven through by the loyal Cromwell, who had made himself the most powerful man in Parliament, which established the monarch's absolute authority in matters temporal and spiritual. Meanwhile astrologers confidently predicted that Anne would be delivered of a boy. The Act of Succession, which became law in 1534, bastardized Princess Mary, and ruled that only Anne's children could inherit the crown. On 7 September 1533, Anne gave birth to a girl, the Princess Elizabeth. It was a sorry anticlimax: Henry didn't even attend the celebrations.

Rome itself was slow to act against Henry.

Perhaps the Pope, Clement VII, knowing that Henry had little sympathy with Lutheranism, hoped he would return to the fold eventually.

Meanwhile Henry decided to strike at opponents both great and small. Bishop Fisher of Rochester was a notably saintly man – he is indeed now a saint. He had fearlessly defended Catherine before Campeggio's commission, and showed no signs of toeing the line now. In 1533 he wrote secretly to Charles V urging him to attack Henry. In April 1534 Thomas More and Fisher were consigned to the Tower on successive days. Henry had decided that prominent men had to take oaths swearing to accept the Act of Supremacy of 1534, by which the monarch gained absolute control of the Church in England, in place of the

Pope, and the Act of Succession. More and Fisher were willing to take the oath of Succession, since they deemed that to be a matter for Parliament to settle. But the oath of Supremacy they refused. Cranmer, hoping to save bloodshed, looked for compromise, but Henry would have none of it. While Fisher and More languished in the Tower, Pope Clement died, and was succeeded by Paul III, who appointed Fisher a Cardinal. It was a gesture of support that cost Fisher his life: Henry resolved that the Pope could have Fisher's head to place a cardinal's hat on it. Fellow prisoners were hung, drawn and quartered on 4 May 1535. Fisher was executed on 22 June 1535, and More on 6 July. The former Lord Chancellor had been sentenced to the traitor's death of being hung, drawn and quartered, but Henry decided to show mercy by having him beheaded. More's wry response was 'God forbid that the King should use any more such mercy to any of my friends'.

Cromwell, appointed Vicar-General by his grateful master, set about masterminding Henry's looting of the Church of which the King was supposedly now the Supreme Head. He drew up a detailed assessment of its wealth. In February 1536 he had a bill introduced to Parliament for the abolition of monasteries with an annual income of less than £200. Having picked off the weaker houses, he could proceed to the greater. By 1540 they were all gone, bringing Henry unprecedented wealth.

Not everyone gave in without a struggle. The Abbot of Glastonbury, flatly refusing to co-operate, was dragged from his abbey and killed. More sustained resistance arose in the north, where monasteries tended to use their wealth to more genuinely charitable ends than in the south. The several simultaneous risings of 1536 are now generally known by one name, the Pilgrimage of Grace. The leaders played their hand according to an old established protocol: the people make known their grievances to the King, on accepting his word that he will redress specific wrongs, they disperse. Unfortunately for them, Henry worked by another code: buy whatever time is needed with concessions, then strike. Thus a rebellion which, had it been set on overthrowing Henry, might have succeeded, was defeated by lies and followed by some 150 executions.

The break with Rome and the dissolution

of the monasteries were the foundations of what would become the Protestant Church of England. They also left Henry richer and more powerful than any previous English monarch. It was not to last.

TROUBLE AND STRIFE

Henry did not enjoy married bliss with
Anne for long. The birth of a daughter
rather than a son did nothing to sweeten his
temper, and by the following year he was
flirting with a young lady at court, Jane
Seymour, the sister of the Duke of
Somerset and a lady-in-waiting to both
Catherine and then Anne. Anne made the
mistake of protesting at this. On one
occasion, even before they were married,
Henry complained to the Duke of Norfolk

that Anne was arrogant towards him, unlike Catherine, 'who never in her life used ill words to him'. Henry's flirtations did nothing to improve matters. Catherine fell ill in December 1535; cruelly, they both celebrated Catherine's death on 7 January 1536. But Anne's miscarriage a few days later infuriated Henry, though she tried to excuse herself by saying that it had been caused by anxiety for Henry's health after a jousting accident. He was a dangerous man to displease, and now started to seek grounds for a divorce. Nothing plausible came to light, so a secret commission under Cromwell and Norfolk was charged that April with investigating Anne's wrongdoings. Anne was no saint, but the evidence of treasonable adultery and incest that was brought against her at her trial the following month strained credulity. Her alleged lovers went to the scaffold on 17 May, and Anne followed them two days later, dispatched, by special dispensation, by an expert swordsman.

In the ten years and some odd months that remained to him, Henry was to marry four more times. But he was no Lothario. It was a long time since he had been the athletic young prince who won the admiration of all Europe. He was bloated, and his legs seeped pus from incurable ulcers. His increasing girth caused the occasional incident, as on one occasion in the 1530s when Henry, eager to show himself as lithe as ever, tried to pole-vault over a stream, only to have the pole snap and catapult him head first into the mud. By the late 1530s his physical condition was deteriorating; his sanity had always been hard to judge.

Jane Seymour

In the same month that Anne was executed, Henry married Jane. She was a modest, dutiful woman, who made some attempt to reconcile Henry with Princess Mary. Her dutifulness extended to bearing Henry a son, Edward, born on 12 October 1537. However, childbirth was a dangerous business and she died twelve days later. Henry at last had the son and heir he craved, but the loss of his third queen may have haunted him. According to one story he died with Jane's name on his lips, and asked to be buried next to her.

A new Act of Succession had bastardized Elizabeth, and conferred on Henry the extraordinary power to appoint his successor. This may have been an attempt to revive the idea of making his illegitimate son by Elizabeth Blount,

Prince Edward, later Edward VI

Henry Fitzroy, his heir. However, Fitzroy had died a few days after the act became law in 1536, and thanks to Jane Seymour Henry at last had a son. The problem he had been struggling to solve for years was solved, at least for the time being. At home, once the Pilgrimage of Grace had been defeated, Henry looked more wealthy and more powerful than ever. He indulged himself in a programme of building, the high point of which was the completion in 1538 of the fabulous palace of Nonsuch in Surrey, but little of it survives. However, internationally he was dangerously isolated. In 1538 Pope Paul III issued a Bull of Deprivation against him, by which all true Christian princes were called upon to depose him. The following year it seemed as if Charles V and Francis I might ally to do precisely that. In urgent need of allies himself, Henry started to explore the international marriage market. He derived much pleasure from comparing and contrasting the attractions of the princesses of Europe, sending out envoys to investigate, and saddling the painter Hans Holbein the Younger with the task of painting likely candidates. The invasion scare passed in due course, but Thomas Cromwell still urged the need to cement an alliance by marriage.

After exploring grander possibilities, some of whom were understandably concerned by Henry's marital record, it was finally decided that the Duchy of Cleves might be a suitable candidate for an ally. The duchy was so placed on the Rhine that it could cause Charles sufficient problems, if matters were to come to that, to make him think twice about angering Henry, and the ruling family also boasted two unmarried daughters. Having heard extravagant praise and having seen Holbein's flattering portrait, Henry decided to marry Anne. Arrangements were made, and Anne arrived in England. At the very end of 1539, Henry dashed eagerly to Rochester to greet his bride with New Year gifts, but when he set eyes on her his heart sank. He found her insuperably ugly. For two days he tried to find a way to get out of the marriage, but it seems likely that Cromwell insisted he go through with it. Within six months Henry was divorcing Anne on the grounds that the marriage had never been consummated. Anne docilely went along with whatever Henry asked, and when all had been arranged, settled down to live in the houses Henry had given her in England.

Anne of Cleves

The divorce was confirmed in July 1540. The preceding month Cromwell had suffered the same fate as Wolsey. It is not clear exactly what caused his fall. Aristocratic resentment and his role in the Cleves marriage probably had some part in it, and it has been suggested that the King was displeased at Cromwell's alleged religious radicalism. At any event, in the same month as Henry was divorced, he had Cromwell executed, and then married for the fifth time.

Catherine Howard was a relation of the Duke of Norfolk (as, distantly, had been Anne Boleyn). She was captivating, wild, and, as it transpired, promiscuous. Hoping to control the King through his libido, Norfolk had trailed his young relation under Henry's nose, and he took the bait. Catherine's upbringing had been loose. She

Catherine Howard

seems to have become accustomed to rather more sexual fulfilment than an obese semi-invalid could supply, and she had no intention of doing without. Evidence was gathered of her backstairs liaisons, and though Henry tried to ignore it, it was irrefutable. Her alleged lovers were executed just before Christmas 1541. On 13 February 1542, she joined them.

Henry was grief-stricken – more, as one observer noted, for his own sake rather than Catherine's. He had prided himself on his physique, but now his infirmities were becoming harder to deny. He returned to the ambition of his youth: to win back English possessions in France. In the summer of 1542, Francis I and Charles V were again at loggerheads, and Henry saw his chance. Norfolk was sent north to deal with the Scots, in anticipation of Henry's leading a force over the Channel. Norfolk routed a superior Scots force at Solway Moss; James V of Scotland was so dismayed he died of grief at the shame of it. The peace treaty of July 1543 provided for marriage between Prince Edward and the infant Mary, Queen of Scots. The path to France ought to have been clear, but the Scots welched on the deal, and only after Henry had ordered savage reprisals in the summer of 1544, did he feel free to embark for Calais.

He arrived there on 14 July. According to an agreement with Charles V, Henry was to march on Paris, while Charles attacked on a second front. Boulogne fell on 18 September, but since Henry showed no sign of moving on Paris, Charles made a separate peace with the French. Henry's impetus flagged; besides, the expedition had proved financially so crippling that it was, at best, a Pyrrhic victory.

Henry returned to England to try to deal with the financial mess for which he was largely responsible. Much of the land he had plundered from the Church was sold off, the currency was debased, but he still had to borrow on the money markets. The solace of his declining years was his sixth and last wife. Catherine Parr was a sensible, devout widow when she married Henry. She set about bringing some semblance of harmony to Henry's tangled family, and even tackled their education. Her one brush with danger came when it was alleged that she was promoting radical religious ideas. She hastened to her

Catherine Parr

husband and submitted wholly to his guidance. Henry beamed with delight, and when Sir Thomas Wriothesley came to arrest the Queen, he found Henry with her, and was sent packing with 'Knave! arrant knave! beast! and fool!'

The King was by now gravely ill, but no less dangerous for that. In 1546, the Duke of Norfolk and his son, the Earl of Surrey, poet and soldier, were arrested. It is hard to know why; but Henry did not always need a reason. Surrey had blotted his military reputation in France, and in addition had universely boasted of his Plantagenet blood. (Henry's father had destroyed the Plantagenet royal succession at Bosworth). Possibly Norfolk's enemies were striking at him through his son. Surrey was executed on 12 December 1546, and the order for

Norfolk's execution was prepared the following month. Before it could be carried out, however, in the small hours of Friday, 28 January 1547, Henry himself finally breathed his last, having received such spiritual comfort as Cranmer could offer him. His death was concealed for three days while Norfolk's fate was debated; he survived. The following month the country formally mourned his death and he was laid to rest with Jane Seymour, the mother of his son and heir. That son, barely ten years old, succeeded him as Edward VI.

FURTHER MINI SERIES
INCLUDE

THEY DIED TOO YOUNG

Elvis
James Dean
Buddy Holly
Jimi Hendrix
Sid Vicious
Marc Bolan
Ayrton Senna
Marilyn Monroe
Jim Morrison

THEY DIED TOO YOUNG

Malcolm X
Kurt Cobain
River Phoenix
John Lennon
Glenn Miller
Isadora Duncan
Rudolph Valentino
Freddie Mercury
Bob Marley

FURTHER MINI SERIES INCLUDE

HEROES OF THE WILD WEST

General Custer
Butch Cassidy and the Sundance Kid
Billy the Kid
Annie Oakley
Buffalo Bill
Geronimo
Wyatt Earp
Doc Holliday
Sitting Bull
Jesse James